DoGGY WhYS

LiLa PraP

We say that dogs are our best friends.
Of course they are—they would do anything for us.
They entertain us, take us for walks, fearlessly
defend us against other dogs and cats. But that's not all.
Dogs guard grazing animals, pull sleds, help the police
catch criminals, rescue injured people, and help the blind
and disabled. And what do they expect from us for all of
this loyalty and unselfishness? Nothing special.
Just to understand them a little better.
Our bulldog will explain a few things about dogs to you.
If there is anything else you would like to know,
just ask your dog!

DoGGY WhYS

LiLa PraP

NorthSouth
New York / London

Because they
don't know
how to use their
own heads.

Because they
can't open a
can of dog food
on their own.

Because they
want people to
like them more
than people
like cats.

Dogs obey their masters because dogs descended from wolves. This is also why dogs feel so attached to their families.

Wolves live in packs, which are a little bit like large families. Each member of the pack has a job. Some are on guard, looking out for danger to the pack. Others take care of the young wolves. Still others find food. The leader of the pack decides what job each member will do.

Thousands of years ago, people began to bring young wolves into their homes. No longer part of a pack of wolves, these wolf pups began to think of the people around them as their packs. The friendliest and most obedient young wolves were chosen for breeding. With each new generation, the pups got friendlier and more obedient. Gradually the frightening wolves turned into the most faithful human companions. But every dog today, no matter how small and sweet, carries within it the pride and courage of its distant ancestors.

THE WEST HIGHLAND WHITE TERRIER

stands under a foot high and weighs less than 25 pounds. In the past, West Highland white terriers were used to hunt otters, foxes, and rats. Today they are extremely friendly and lively pets, but also alert and noisy guard dogs. If they don't get enough attention and are not taught good behavior, they will chase every animal and object they see.

ell THem?

Because they all forgot that they are supposed to look like wolves.

Because each of them wants to look like its owner.

Because each of them wants to be something special.

The domesticated descendants of wolves had different characteristics. Some were good at hunting. Others barked very loudly and made good guard dogs. Still others were better at bringing home a herd of sheep or watching over children.

Gradually people realized that parents with similar qualities produced puppies in which those qualities were even stronger. Two good guard dogs were likely to produce even better guard dogs. Two large dogs would produce other large dogs. Temperament, size, length of hair, and even spots of color could be passed on to create new breeds.

The DALMATIAN

was first used as a hunting dog. Later, Dalmatians were taken along on horse-drawn coaches to protect the passengers from highway robberies. Today Dalmatians are popular family pets. They are very attached to their families and get along well with children; but if they are not used to meeting people, they are not always friendly. They are very energetic and need lots of exercise.

Because they are beaten.

Because they expect a treat.

Because they are stupid.

How obedient a dog is depends on its owner, especially on how much attention and teaching the owner gives the dog. Some breeds are more receptive to training than others. Sheepdogs, for example, must carry out a lot of complicated maneuvers in order to herd and look after a flock of sheep. To do this, they must learn a number of human words and signs. For other dogs that guard flocks on their own or hunting dogs that have to use their heads while pursuing wild animals, learning different human commands isn't as useful. However, every dog can be taught a few words. You can teach dogs during play or by showing them what a word means.

The COLLIE

is one of the easiest dogs to teach. Collies make excellent sheepdogs. They are also used as guard dogs and as guide dogs for the blind, and to rescue people from water or fire. And they do well as military and police dogs too. Many people keep collies as pets, but unless they are properly raised, you cannot teach them even the basic commands.

Why Do Dogs Bark?

Because they think it's fun to frighten people.

Because they don't know how to meow.

Because they like the sound of their own voices.

Dogs bark because they have something to say. A loud, continuous bark warns members of a dog's family that something is happening—for example, "We have a visitor!" or "A car is driving past the house!" A slightly different bark might mean "I'm thirsty!" or "Why have you left me alone?"

When a dog is lonely or when a male dog can't get to a good-looking female dog, he may start to howl.

Barking accompanied by growling and the baring of teeth might mean "I don't like you at all. Don't come near me until one of my family comes!"

Compared to wolves, dogs bark much louder and longer without interruption—though there are some dogs that cannot bark or bark only rarely.

ALASKAN MALAMUTEs

are rarely heard barking. They were used by Eskimos for hunting, guarding herds of caribou, and pulling dogsleds. Today they are popular family dogs. They are gentle and kind with humans and make devoted companions, but they are not friendly to dogs they don't know. They like to run and play, and they love to be talked to. They respond with a kind of squeak.

Why Do DogS GrOwl?

Because they've swallowed a buzzing alarm clock.

They're not growling —they're gargling to soothe a sore throat.

Because they have a tummy ache.

A dog growls when it feels threatened. "Go away or I might bite you!" it is warning.

Growling is also a sign that a dog is afraid. The louder the growl, the more it is trying to drive the intruder away without a fight. When a dog switches between growling and barking, it would like to drive someone away (*grrrr*) and it would like the help of other members of its pack (*woof woof woof*).

The CHiHuAHUA

is the smallest breed of dog in the world. It is renowned for its fighting spirit, and many tend to growl and bark a lot. (You might growl and bark too if you were just 10 inches tall in a world of giants!) But Chihuahuas can be taught to behave nicely; and they are lively, smart, and very loyal to their owners.

Why Do Dogs Wag Their Tails?

Because they
like to
show off.

To shake
off fleas.

To cool
themselves.

Tail wagging is a kind of doggy smile. Puppies don't begin to wag their tails until they are about two months old. At that age they are old enough to start fighting with their brothers and sisters for their mother's teats. Wagging their tails means something like "Ooops. Excuse me. No offense!"

Pups a bit older might wag their tails when they meet someone new. "Hi there. Are we friends or not?" their tails are saying. Most puppies and dogs wag their tails to say "Welcome home!" or "Let's play!" or "I'm happy!"

A wagging tail raised high and kept stiff can mean that a dog is ready to attack. Timid dogs encountering this will wag their tails as low as they can.

The POODLE

is an enthusiastic tail wagger. Poodles are lively, happy, even-tempered dogs. They were initially bred to hunt waterfowl, and they are good swimmers. Later they became popular with ladies at royal courts, and it's probably those ladies who came up with the idea of giving poodles fancy haircuts. Poodles are intelligent and eager to learn, which are traits that make them popular circus dogs.

Because they
don't know
what a tail
is for.

To make the
dog shorter.

So that
the tail won't
get caught in
doors.

Dogs' Tails?

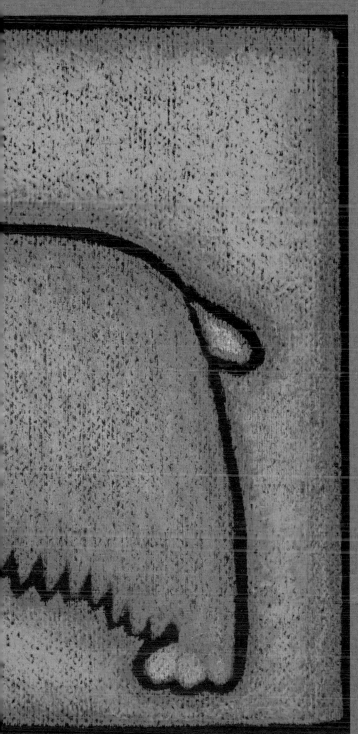

Some people think a tail stump is more attractive on some dogs, so they cut off part of the tail. We say those tails are "docked." Tail docking was started by the ancient Romans, who thought that the worms that cause rabies lived on dogs' tails. Even though later that was proven wrong, tail docking has continued. Why?

Just over 150 years ago, dog lovers began organizing dog shows. Prizes were given to the dogs that the judges thought looked the best. The judges thought that the tails and ears of some dogs didn't look as elegant as the rest of the dog, so they decided that these breeds should have their tails and ears docked. Today this custom is starting to be abandoned.

The COCKER SPANIEL

is a breed that people find more attractive without a tail. Cockers are still popular hunting dogs, able both to flush out and retrieve birds. They are also popular house pets. Lively and playful, cockers have been called "merry cockers" because of their tireless tail wagging—that is, if not too much of the dog's tail tail has been cut off.

Why Do Dogs Sniff Each Other?

Because they are dirty creatures.

They can't tell the head from the bottom.

To see if the other dog sat in something smelly.

Bottoms?

Special glands in a dog's bottom produce a multitude of smells. These smells are like a dog's business card and can tell other dogs a number of things, such as "I'm a very friendly fellow, and at this moment I don't want to fight" or "I'm a little nervous today because I have indigestion" or "I'm top dog around here" or "I'm a classy lady, so please leave me alone."

Two dogs of equal rank will sniff each other with their tails raised high. Timid dogs will hide their business cards by pressing their tails between their legs.

The BULL TERRIER

is not very enthusiastic about letting other dogs sniff its bottom. Bull terriers were bred for dog fights, and their bite is among the worst dog bites of all. As pets, they are very friendly toward children and loyal to their owners, but they are mistrustful of strangers and do not care much for other dogs either.

They are doing ballet exercises.

To show off.

Because they have a cramp in their leg.

Just like people, dogs have many ways to send messages and make announcements. One of these ways is by peeing. A dog will pee in some obvious place, leaving a message behind. Other dogs read the message by sniffing it. It might say "Around here I'm the boss!" or "I'm the best-looking, strongest dog around, and I'm looking for a doggy girlfriend!" or "Fifi was here!" Since they want to leave messages that are as "fragrant" and long lasting as possible, dogs lift their legs as high as they can when they are peeing.

Every dog that passes a doggy message wants to comment on it. Some smaller dogs will even roll on their backs because they are trying so hard to add to the message that went before.

Only adult males lift their hind legs to pee. Female dogs and puppies squat instead. Only rarely will a female left her leg.

The BULLDOG

is a breed that has to lift its leg quite high. Today's bulldogs are descendants of dogs trained to fight bulls. When this kind of fighting was banned, bulldogs became family pets. They are gentle and good-natured and love children.

Why Do Some Dogs Have

It hurts less when they fall.

They forgot how to grow.

They're scared of heights.

...hort Legs?

Dogs with short legs were bred this way for two reasons: 1. Short-legged dogs stepped awkwardly, like toys, which entertained the nobility and their children, and 2. Dogs with short legs could squeeze into underground tunnels and flush out animals hiding there for hunters.

The DACHSHUND

accompanies hunters who are after foxes and badgers. With its very short legs, it can squeeze into any burrow and drive out the animal that is hidden there. The dachsund is also a popular family pet. It is curious and lively, but also sometimes stubborn. It loves to play and is happiest when someone pulls it by the tail or the ear for fun.

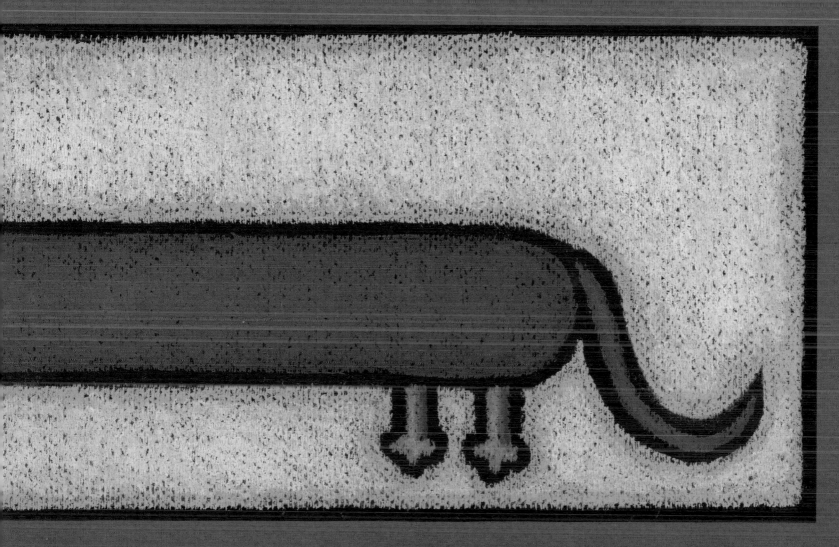

So they don't have to listen to annoying owners.

Because they're too lazy to hold them up.

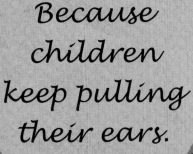

Because children keep pulling their ears.

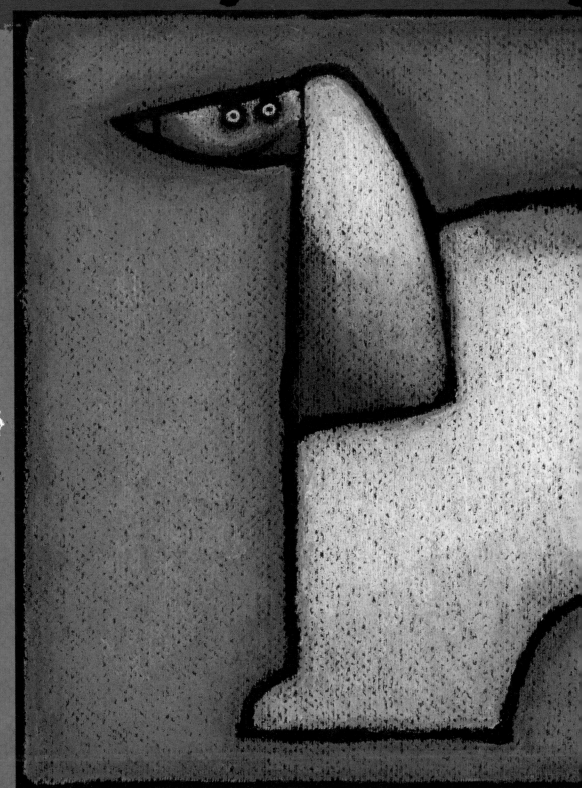

Dogs have very good hearing and can hear sounds that the human ear cannot. Dogs with droopy ears can hear just as well as dogs with short ears, but they can't tell from which direction the sound is coming. Some kinds of hunting dog have been bred with hanging ears so that when they are tracking, they can concentrate on sniffing without being distracted by different noises. Because they look friendlier than dogs with pointed ears, dogs with flapping ears are very popular house pets.

The AFGHAN HOUND

has ears that are so long and covered with hair that the dog looks as if it has a woman's hairdo. Afghan hounds were originally bred in Persia (Iran), where they were used to hunt leopards, wolves, and jackals. They are lively and affectionate pets, but they are quickly offended if they do not get enough attention.

Because they are badly brought up.

Because their tongues are too long.

To catch flies when they are hungry.

ues?

When we are hot we sweat. Perspiring cools us off. Horses and some other animals also sweat. But dogs have sweat glands only in their footpads and cannot cool down through their skin. So when it's hot, dogs cool down by sticking out their tongues and panting. Dogs also stick out their tongues when they are excited. Show them a piece of their favorite salami or their favorite ball and you will see!

The PEKINGESE

has a thick coat and short legs, so it must often stick out its tongue to cool off. In the past, this dog was prized in the Chinese imperial court as a sacred animal that would drive off evil spirits. When an emperor died, all of his Pekingese were killed so they could accompany him to the next life. When the imperial palace was attacked more than 150 years ago, the imperial guards were ordered to kill all of the emperor's dogs in order to stop them from falling into the hands of foreigners. The foreign soldiers managed to rescue five Pekingese, from which all of today's Pekingese are descended.

Today the Pekingese is a popular pet, but it hasn't forgotten its royal past. It is good with adults and children; but it is also proud, has a mind of its own, and likes to be spoiled.

So the cats don't get too lazy.

Because  they want to play tag.

Because they  are in love with cats.

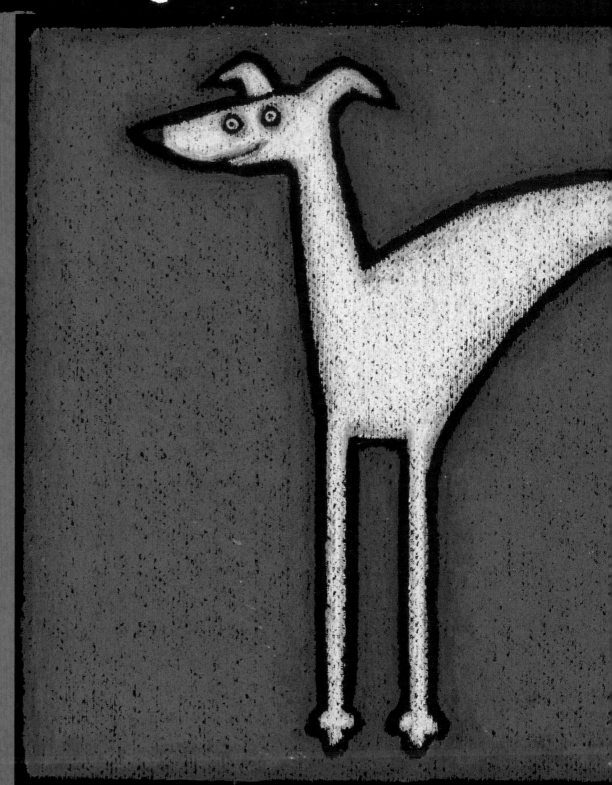

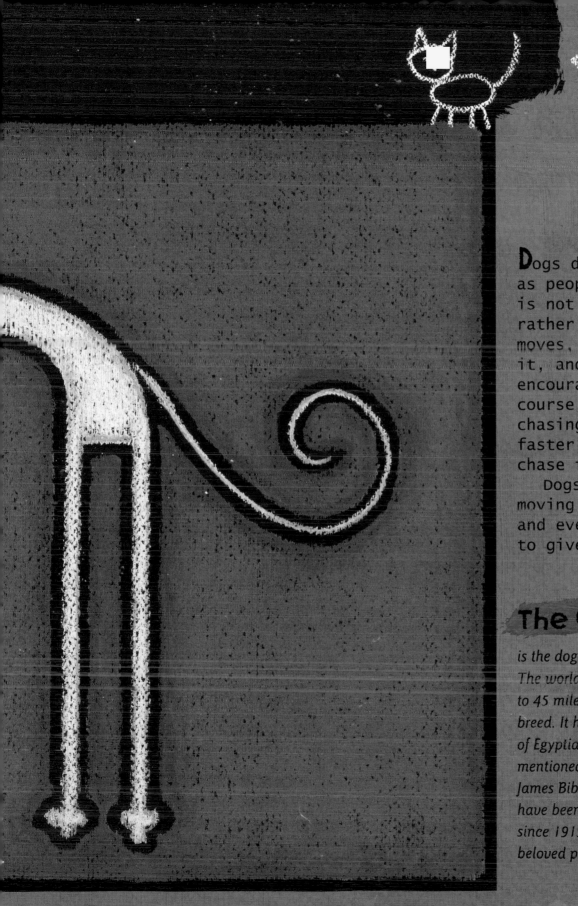

Dogs do not see as many colors as people see, so their attention is not attracted by color but rather by movement. When a cat moves, a dog is sure to notice it, and the dog's hunting instinct encourages it to give chase. Of course, when a cat sees a dog chasing it, the cat runs even faster, which prompts the dog to chase faster.

Dogs aren't only interested in moving cats. Rabbits, chickens, and even people can encourage them to give chase.

The GREYHOUND

is the dog most known for running after things. The world's fastest dog, it can reach speeds of up to 45 miles per hour. The greyhound is an ancient breed. It has been depicted on the walls of the tombs of Egyptian pharaohs, and it is the only dog to be mentioned in the Bible (Proverbs 30: 29-31, King James Bible). Originally hunting dogs, greyhounds have been used as racing dogs in the United States since 1919. Gentle and smart, they have been beloved pets for centuries.

They don't like the way they are dressed.

They think they are show-offs.

They do like them—for a meal!

People?

Like people, dogs are mistrustful of strangers that enter their "territory." Uncertain and hesitant visitors only increase this mistrust, especially if the visitor starts to run away.

People who know how to deal with dogs can quickly calm even the loudest barking pet. In a calm, relaxed way, they come closer and introduce themselves with a gentle touch. Of course you can only get to know a dog in this way if it is jumping up and down and wagging its tail. If the dog is standing rigidly, growling, and baring its teeth, or is just silently staring at you, it is best to wait until the dog's owner appears. Luckily, such aggressive dogs are rare. Most dogs are easily befriended.

The FOX TERRIER

likes to bark at visitors but is not hard to befriend. Fox terriers were carried into the hunt in a basket on horseback and then released when a fox's den was discovered. Fox terriers make friendly, lively pets, but they can be stubborn if things don't go their way. They have a strong hunting instinct and will chase anything that moves.

Many people have mixed-breed dogs—dogs that are half cocker spaniel and half poodle, for example. Actually, there is a new breed that is exactly that—it's called a cockapoo, and it has become a very popular pet.

It's fun to imagine what a new mixed breed might look like, and Lila Prap has done just that on the endpapers of this book. See if you can spot her new mixed-breed inventions! (None of these mixed breeds exist in real life.) Then go ahead and invent some new mixed breeds of your own!

Are you thinking of getting a dog as a pet? Great! We are man's best friend. But if you don't want a dog that will simply lie down on a walk and have to be carried home, or if a dog that keeps drooling, snoring, and occasionally letting off smelly farts will get on your nerves, then don't choose me! There are plenty of other dogs waiting for you at breeders or with neighbors or people you know. And if you'd like to make one of the unhappiest creatures in the world happy, visit your nearest animal shelter.

ANSWERS: AFGHAN SPANIEL, BULLFOXER, BULLMATIAN, BULLMUTE, BULLOODLE, CHISPANIEL, COCKERHOUND, COCKEROODLE, COCKER TERRIER, COLLIEHOUND, COLLIEMUTE, DACHSCHAN, DACHSLAND TERRIOR, DALMACOLLIE, DALMASPANIEL, FOODLE, FOXHUAHUA, FOXOODLE, GREYOODLE, HIGHCHUAHUA, PEKINHUND, WEST HIGHLAND DACHSHUND, WEST HIGHLAND DALMATIAN, WEST HIGHLAND GREYHOUND

POODLE

AFGHAN SPANIEL

CHIHUAHUA

BULL TERRIER

FOXHUAHUA

DACHSHUND

WEST HIGHLAND
WHITE TERRIER

PEKINGESE

COLLIE

WEST HIGHLAND GREYHOUND

BULLDOG

COCKER SPANIEL

AFGHAN HOUND

FOXOODLE

ALASKAN MALAMUTE

FOX TERRIER

GREYOODLE

COLLIE

BULLDOG

COCKER SPANIEL

PEKINHUND

DALMATIAN

WEST HIGHLAND DACHSHUND

CHIHUAHUA

POODLE

PEKINGESE

COLLIEHOUND

ALASKAN MALAMUTE

WEST HIGHLAND WHITE TERRIER